CW00794396

For Christina Wilson

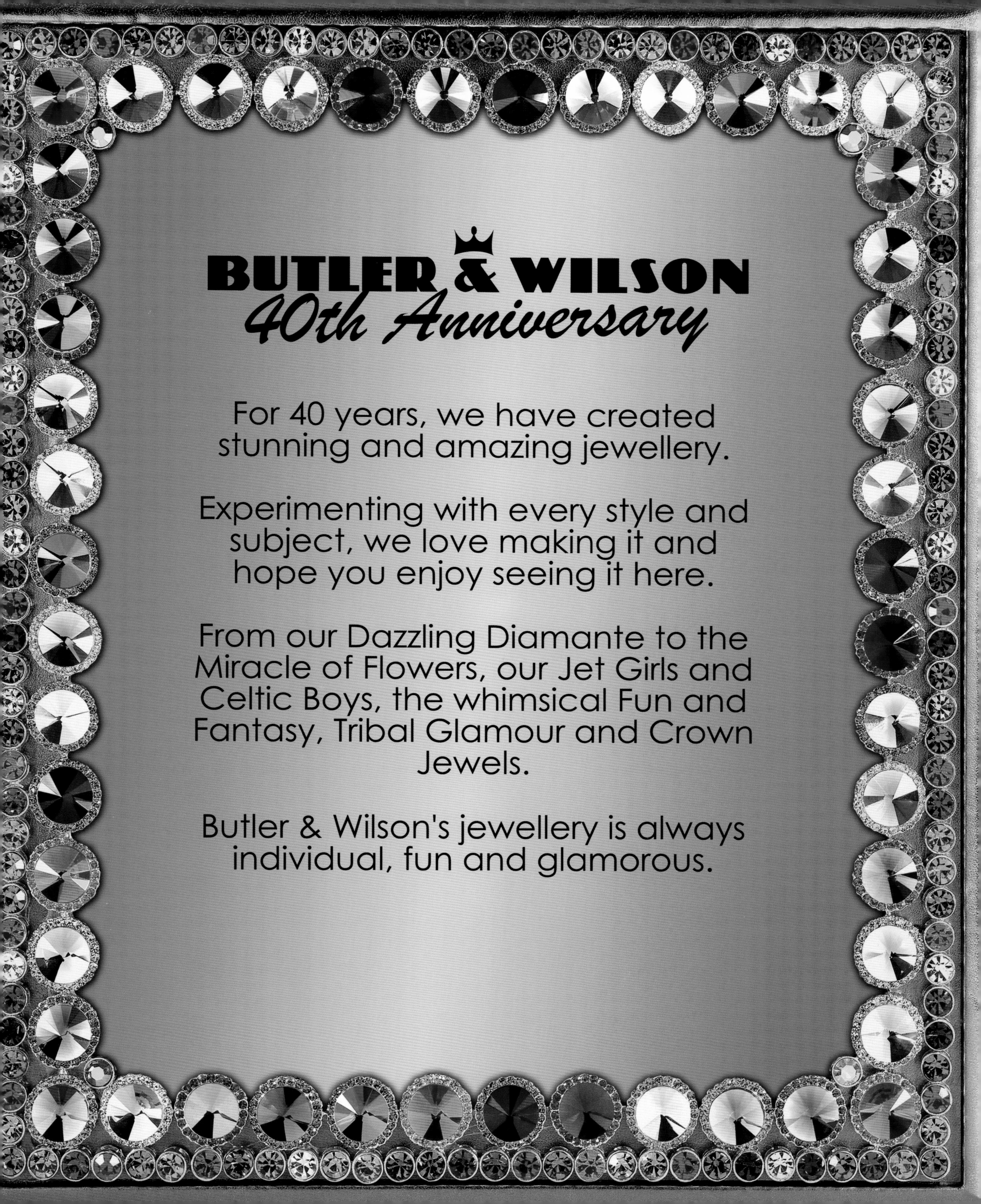

BUTLER & WILSON
40th Anniversary

For 40 years, we have created stunning and amazing jewellery.

Experimenting with every style and subject, we love making it and hope you enjoy seeing it here.

From our Dazzling Diamante to the Miracle of Flowers, our Jet Girls and Celtic Boys, the whimsical Fun and Fantasy, Tribal Glamour and Crown Jewels.

Butler & Wilson's jewellery is always individual, fun and glamorous.

DAZZLING DIAMANTE

"Modern jewellery was really dull in the late 1970s," remembers Simon Wilson. "You either wore a little diamond pendant with matching studs or it was plastic popper beads. That was the only choice! There was a gap in the market and we decided to fill it by creating our first original designs. Our attitude was let's make it bigger, let's make it bolder, let's dress it up and makes a statement with our accessories. We produced these huge, outrageous pieces in diamante. Somehow they just felt right for the times and I really think it was us who introduced that 80s sense of glamour into jewellery".

Butler & Wilson transformed costume jewellery from a cheap alternative into high fashion, and the stone that epitomised the shiny, 'Look at me' 1980s was diamante.

Made from glass, diamante (also known as paste or rhinestones) has a long history of making people look fabulous. For centuries jewellers had used rock crystal to emulate diamonds (the large quartz deposits found around the Rhine river inspired the name rhinestone) but when British glass maker George Ravenscroft perfected lead glass in the 1670s, he not only changed drinking habits, but jewellery.

This new lead crystal was clearer, more brilliant and less fragile than Venetian soda glass. Easier to work than quartz, it could be facetted, polished and tinted, making it the perfect substitute for diamonds and coloured gems.

By the 1700s, paste jewellery was being worn not only by the middle classes who could not afford the real thing, but by the rich. What with highwaymen and footpads (the muggers of the 18th century), travelling was a risky business and many ladies preferred to leave their valuables at home but still wanted to sparkle at court.

George Frederic Strass (1701-73), jeweller to Louis XV, created paste jewellery for royal mistress Mme Du Barry, and all the leading beauties of Versailles, with his creations becoming so famous that "Strass" became yet another synonym for diamante.

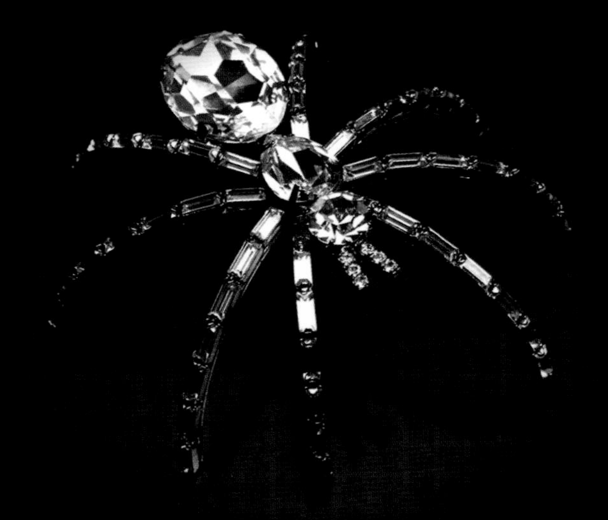

18th century paste was highly prized, beautifully crafted and something to show off in public. In the Victorian period, quality declined and paste was predominantly used to provide discreet copies of real jewellery, but in the 20th century, diamante once again became an art form in its own right.

In 1892, Bohemian jeweller Daniel Swarovski patented a new machine for mass producing cut glass stones. The process was refined in the 1900s, and by the roaring twenties, Swarovski crystals were being exported across the world. Diamante was the perfect decoration for the Jazz Age.

Josephine Baker took Paris by storm and charlestoned on to the stage wearing nothing but a tail of ostrich feathers and sparkling rhinestone jewellery. A new generation of flappers cast off their corsets, shingled their hair, and festooned daringly short dresses, with crystal beads and diamante fringes. All white jewellery became the latest Art Deco look and Cartier's diamond dress clips and geometric bracelets were reproduced in affordable paste.

The new generation of couturiers helped make costume jewellery acceptable to even their smartest clients. Coco Chanel led the way in the 1930s, and accessorised her classic, simple outfits, with magnificent costume jewellery modelled on the Romanov jewels given to her by her lover the Grand Duke Dimitri of Russia. Schiaparelli's jewellery was inspired by Dada and surrealism and designed by leading artists of the day.

In the fifties, Christian Dior designed jewellery collections to complement his New Look fashions and popularised Swarovski's Aurora Borealis: rhinestones tinted iridescent rainbow colours that epitomised the post war desire for fantasy and femininity.

With the end of the seventies came a period of transformation. Lady Diana Spencer mutated from 'Shy Di' into a fairytale princess; Stuart Goddard changed his name to Adam Ant and became Prince Charming; Joan Collins reinvented herself as Dynasty's Alexis Carrington, the stylish queen of mean. All of them shopped at Butler & Wilson, where flamboyant diamante turned everyone into a star.

"The word that sums up the 80s was glamour. This was jewellery that went with huge shoulder pads, shiny taffeta ball gowns and that whole Dynasty power trip. It was big, it was show off, it was fabulous and I loved it."

Big, beautiful, witty, sometimes shocking but always stylish, Butler & Wilson's jewellery encapsulated the powerful femininity of a decade dominated by strong female icons from Margaret Thatcher to Madonna.

The most glamorous women in the world shopped at Butler & Wilson, and queued up to star in the famous posters that appeared on a giant billboard outside their Fulham Road store and that could literally stop the traffic.

Catherine Deneuve, Charlotte Rampling, Fay Dunaway, Marie Helvin, Jerry Hall, along with many other celebrities, were draped with jewellery and photographed by the leading photographers of the day including David Bailey, Robert Mapplethorpe, Helmut Newton and Terry O'Neill.

What these posters underlined was that in the 1980s, Butler & Wilson made flamboyant fakes trendier than real gemstones. Though many of their clients could afford diamonds, what they wanted was exciting designs in diamante.

"I'll never forget a New York client who spent £10,000 on a dress to wear at her daughter's wedding and then bought one of our huge spider brooches to pin on her shoulder. She phoned me after the party. 'I just had to tell you Simon. Nobody noticed the dress. The one thing everybody commented on was the spider!'"

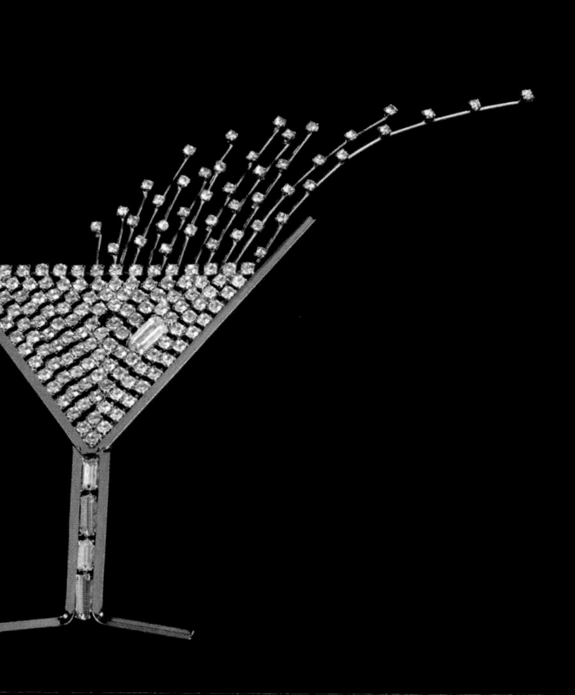

The 1990s saw a new direction for the fashio world. "Fashion died at the beginning of the 90s. During the recession, it was all about grunge, gloom and dressing down. There wa a big reaction against shiny 80s glamour and everything was either black and minimalist o dark and grubby - that depressing heroin ch look. And then suddenly in the mid-90s, you began to see colour, really bright colours, clashing colours, yellow, orange, pink, purpl all mixed together. It was fabulous!"

"For the first time I began making really colourful jewellery. The 80s were all black an white: diamante crystal and jet. Now I was using huge stones like giant sweets in these amazing cocktail colours: fuchsia, turquoise, emerald, scarlet, and tangerine. It was so exciting – it was like opening up a fabulous box of jewels, and I've never looked back."

"When you're designing it's about feeling rather than thought, and somehow tapping to the mood of the moment. Today I'm making huge multicoloured necklaces; headdresses glowing with brilliant stones; brooches and bracelets in amazing fluorescent colours."

"I think we're living in very interesting times. I not like the past when fashion was controlle by Paris and everything was much more formal. Today people get their ideas from al over the world; they mix together eastern an western styles, they combine vintage with modern clothes and high street fashion with designer. They wear what they want, when they want. I don't think we are afraid of colo anymore and I look at all these bright powe colours and they feel right."

Today, Butler & Wilson's 21st century designs are featured in all the major magazines and are attracting a new generation of celebrity enthusiasts ranging from the latest rock stars young royals. In jewellery, as in fashion, age barriers have broken down over the past twenty years. "Now I'm getting the children women who first shopped with me in the 80s doesn't matter what age you are. An amazi piece of diamante will always make you loo and feel great."

"It's not just about dressing up a ball gown a more. People might wear a diamante necklace with a pair of jeans, or pin a huge brooch onto a leather jacket. Attitudes are much more relaxed and style is much less formal than it was in the 80s."

Some things however haven't changed. "Ou jewellery has always been about self-expression, not following the crowd and creating an individual look." Today, as in the past, when you put on a piece of Butler & Wilson, it is jewellery that gets you noticed.

SEXY
RICH
SINGLE
MARRIED

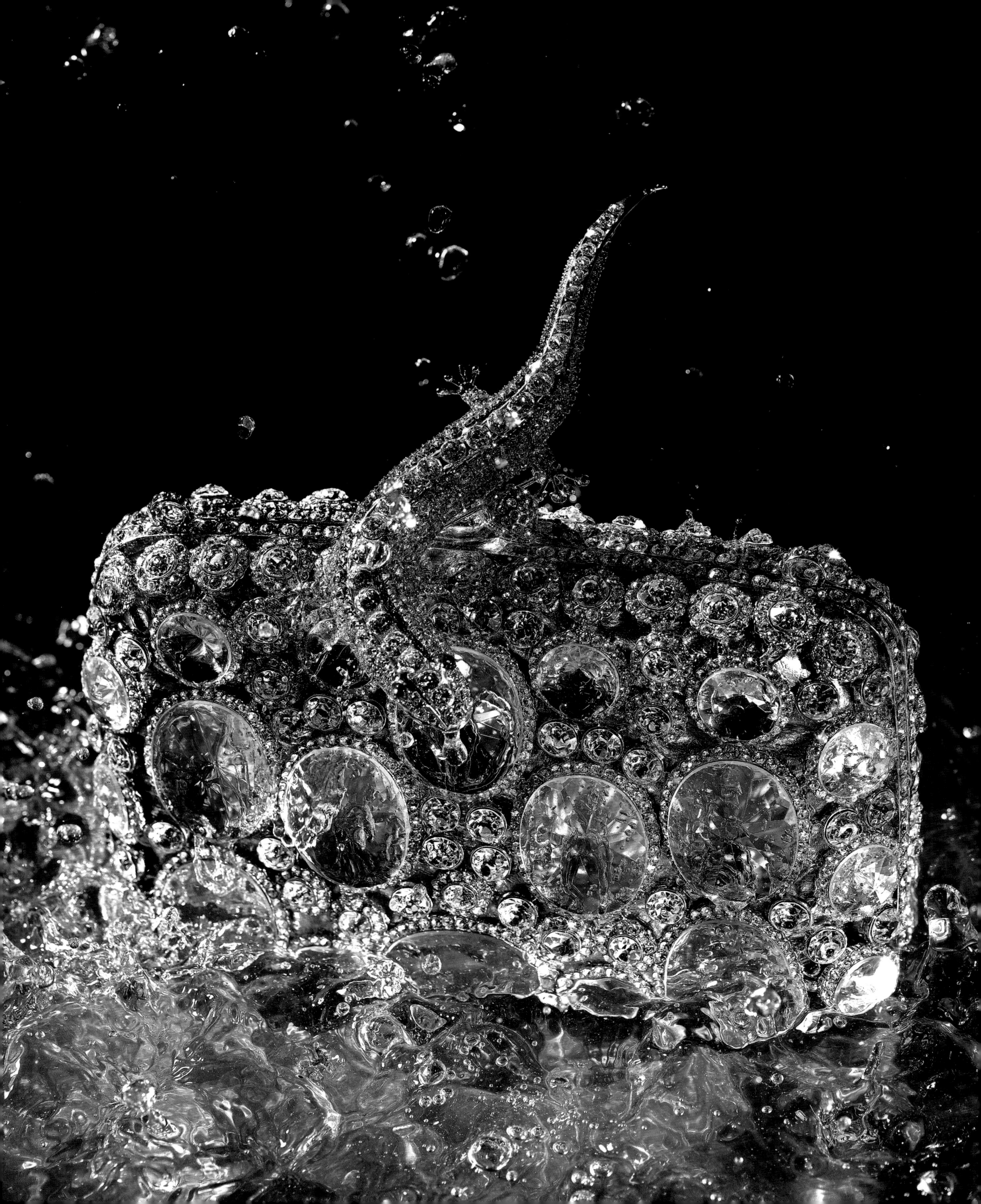

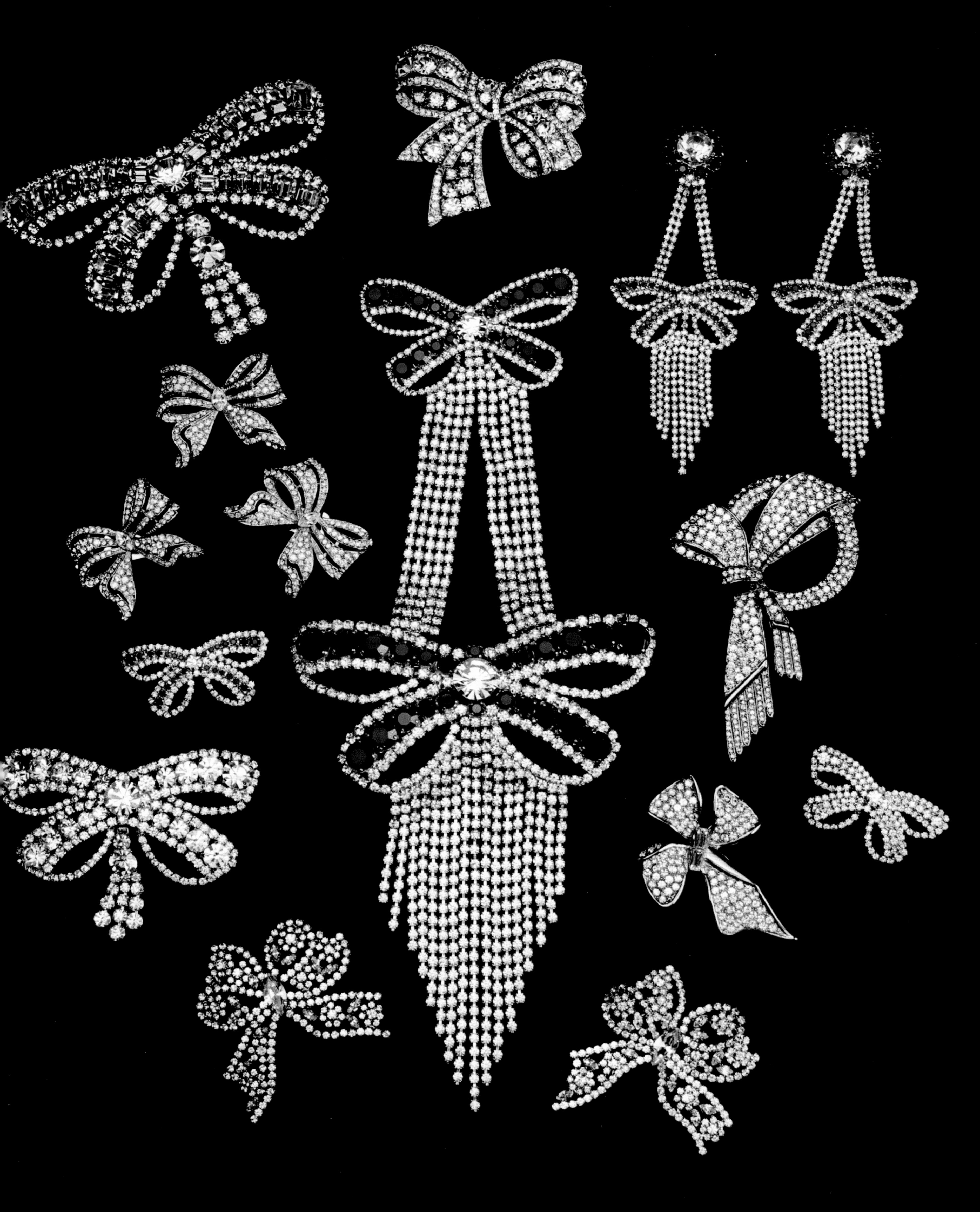

THE MIRACLE OF FLOWERS

"Our jewellery has always been inspired by flowers and nature. Wherever you go in the world you will always see beautiful flowers. It could be purple heather in Scotland; lotus flowers in Thailand or an English rose garden. No matter how many times you see these plants, you never get tired of looking at them. They are always amazing, they make you gasp and that's the feeling that I want to recreate in jewellery. Fashion is always trying to dictate whether florals should be in or out this year but I never take any notice. Flowers have been in fashion forever! Their beauty is timeless and they do make you believe in miracles."

Throughout history flowers have been sacred to every culture. Rooted in mud, rising through water to reach the sunlight and producing a perfect, stainless flower, the lotus is venerated across the East as a manifestation of the creation myth and a symbol of man's journey from earthly materialism, through purification, to spiritual enlightenment.

According to Buddhist mythology, Buddha was born with the ability to walk and as he took his first steps the lotus bloomed for the first time to protect the tender soles of his feet. Like Hindu Gods, Buddha is often depicted sitting on a giant lotus, and the flower is represented in temples and across the decorative arts.

"We have lotus blossoms painted on the walls in our shops and Asian arts have had a huge impact on our floral designs. We might get an idea from the blossoms embroidered on an antique kimono or the gilded sculpture of a buddha, but it's not just about finding amazing images that we can translate into jewellery, it's about recreating a feeling. What I love about these Asian objects, is what I love about flowers: they are decorative, they can be dramatic, but they are also very serene."

Roses are another important image in Butler & Wilson jewellery, and a favourite flower in Western art. In antiquity the rose, because of its beauty and fragrance, was sacred to Venus, Goddess of love, with the thorns symbolizing the pain of love. In Christian iconography, the flower was associated with Mary "a Rose without Thorns". The white rose stood for virginal purity, but a red rose represented the martyr's blood and the word rosary comes from the Latin rosarium, meaning rose garden.

While the French kings adopted the "Fleur de Lys", the golden lily, as their symbol, the rose was the badge of British royalty. After the War of the Roses, when the victorious Henry VII, head of the House of Lancaster, married Elizabeth of York in 1486, the Lancastrian white rose was superimposed onto the red rose of York to create the Tudor Rose, the heraldic emblem of England.

"Flower power didn't just happen in the 60s! Flowers are always powerful. We use them to celebrate marriage and to commemorate death. Throughout history they have always inspired artists and jewellers."

In the 18th and 19th centuries, there was a fashion for remarkable brooches and hair ornaments - huge bouquets of mixed flowers in which diamonds, rubies, emeralds, and gems of every colour were used to simulate the natural beauty of petals and leaves.

"Exotic plants were very valuable so you celebrated them in precious stones. This was the jewellery worn by queens and royal mistresses like Mme de Pompadour. With our big flower necklaces we wanted to recreate that sense of magnificence for the modern age - remarkable flowers, made from beautiful crystals, and designed to make women look amazing."

Like flowers themselves, floral jewellery has always been a favourite romantic gift. The Victorians developed a complex language of flowers, in which each bloom had a specific meaning. The turquoise forget-me-not was a popular image in jewellery; as was the pansy, which, evolving from the French "pensee" (thought), signified 'I think of you'.

Mixing various plants spelt out different messages, and in jewellery these were emphasised by another Victorian conceit – the language of stones. As with flowers, each gemstone was given a specific attribute: - diamond: eternity; ruby: passion; emerald: hope. Create a rose out of diamonds and rubies and the sentiment expressed was eternal, passionate love.

"Jewellers and designers interpret flowers differently in every period. In the 1950s you get skirts covered with giant cabbage roses. In the 60s it was the Mary Quant daisy. In the 70s Laura Ashley revived milkmaid dresses and Victorian floral chintz. Now Butler & Wilson are making floral jewellery that's right for today. Flowers are always fresh and each generation sees them in a new way. How could they ever go out of fashion?"

JET GIRLS

"Black is incredibly chic, but it's also very powerful. And nothing is blacker or more powerful than jet." Jet was one of the first gems to be discovered by man and from the earliest times it was regarded as a hugely potent talisman. A variety of fossilized wood or coal, jet is light in weight, warm to the touch and comes in two types: hard jet which is older, more durable, and perfect for carving; and soft jet, which is more recent and as such more fragile. Colour ranges from brown to the deepest black, and what made it appear so magical long before the age of glass, is that it could be polished to a mirror like sheen and that when rubbed it created static electricity, picking up dust and chaff.

Prehistoric people wore jet amulets to ward off evil spirits and were buried in black jewellery to protect them in the afterlife. The Ancient Greeks believed that jet repelled plague and guarded travellers from danger. According to the Roman naturalist Pliny, the fumes from burnt jet would "keep serpents at a distance and dispel hysterical affections". They could also, he added, detect a tendency to epilepsy and act as a test of virginity.

And of course, jet looked great. Whitby on the North Yorkshire coast was a major source for this valuable material, with jewellery and artefacts made from Whitby jet exported across the Roman Empire.

With the collapse of Rome, demand for jet plummeted. In the Middle Ages the black material was principally used for rosaries and religious ornaments and it wasn't until the mid 19th century that jet jewellery once again became a secular fashion, partly thanks to a royal tragedy.

In 1861, shortly after the death of her mother, Queen Victoria lost her beloved husband Prince Albert when he was only 42, and plunged into the deepest, darkest mourning for most of her remaining life. This was not unusual. The combination of high mortality rates and strict social etiquette meant that Victorian women could spend years dressed in black, but even if they were restricted to crepe and bombazine, they still wanted to look glamorous. The rules of mourning were strict, but did permit black jewellery.

Jet could be beautifully carved and was light enough to produce the huge bracelets and necklaces necessary to set off billowing crinolines.

Jet became the height of fashion and the Whitby industry grew from two shops in 1832, to 200 shops in 1872.

The popularity of jet also spawned demand for other black jewellery including French jet. Made from black glass, it was affordable and easy to mass produce, which, whilst it might have been more fragile than the real thing, was perfect for making beads and dress trimmings.

Black jewellery was a high Victorian favourite. With the end of the 19th century and the death of the old Queen however, tastes changed, and the fashion for elaborate mourning outfits and heavy jet decoration came to an abrupt end. Women turned with relief to light colours, less voluminous dresses, and delicate, art nouveau style jewellery. The Whitby industry fell into a decline and never recovered.

Like much other Victorian design, jet jewellery was to remain unfashionable and largely ignored for three quarters of a century, until it was rediscovered by a new generation of collectors and antique dealers, including Butler & Wilson.

In the 1980s, Simon bought a huge archive collection of jet jewellery from Britain's leading historical expert in the field. "I fell in love with the texture of jet and that lovely dull black sheen. Black and white were the colours of the 80s and looking at all those big, strong Victorian pieces, I realized that we could update them."

Using vintage design as their springboard, Butler & Wilson breathed new life into jet and transformed this Victorian mourning jewellery into the ultimate modern party wear.

They filled the window of their Fulham Road shop with coal in order to display his new range of jet jewellery: gleaming black chokers; huge decorative crosses; row upon row of shining beads; heavy bangles and bracelets worn four or five on each arm.

"The more you put on the better it looked. Our black jewellery wasn't about mourning and it certainly wasn't dusty, sad or old fashioned. It was contemporary, elegant, and dramatic. It made women look powerful and deeply, darkly sexy."

CELTIC BOYS

"I was born and bred in Glasgow. My dad Hector Wilson was a piper in the Black Watch regiment. When you're Scottish, you grow up with tartan. It's not a fashion thing; its part of your culture, part of your national pride. And Scottish jewellery belongs to the same tradition."

In highland dress, it's men that are the peacocks. Richly coloured tartan kilts and plaids are matched by beautiful silverwork: decorated buckles, badges and buttons; finely mounted sporrans and daggers and a range of handsome brooches.

The shoulder brooch - used to secure a cloak or plaid over the chest - is one of the earliest forms of jewellery. Ring shaped brooches and fibulae (safety pin style fasteners) had been worn by Celtic clansmen for over 2000 years, when suddenly in the Victorian age, they became the latest look in ladies' jewellery, partly thanks to the Queen.

Victoria and Albert made their first visit to Scotland in 1842, and were entranced. Six years later they chose Balmoral Castle as their regular summer retreat and Victoria's love for the highlands lasted throughout her life.

"The solitude, the romance and wild loveliness of everything here, the absence of hotels and beggars, the independent simple people, who all speak Gaelic here, all make beloved Scotland the proudest, finest country in the world," she wrote in her journals. "Every year my heart becomes more fixed on this dear paradise."

Scottish jewellery provided a romantic, and affordable, vision of Celtic history, and satisfied two other Victorian interests: a passion for geology and archaeology. Silver brooches and bracelets were inlaid with multicoloured local agates (known as Scotch pebbles) and other native stones such as Cairngorms, the smoky yellow quartz found in the Cairngorm Mountain Range.

Designs were inspired by ancient prototypes and weapons. Popular shapes included the annular shoulder brooch and kilt pin modelled as swords, dirks (the dagger worn at the waist in highland dress), and the skean dhu (the Scottish knife carried in the stocking).

Another favourite motif was the strap and buckle, which traditionally surrounded the emblem of the clan's chieftain, but which also reflected Queen Victoria's role as head of the Order of the Garter.

Edinburgh was the main centre of production but as the craze for Scottish jewellery spread across Europe, it was also manufactured in Birmingham, where standard Victorian designs (anchors and butterfly brooches; large flexible bracelets) were reproduced in the Celtic style.

In the 20th century, although Scottish jewellery remained part of traditional Highland dress, it all but disappeared from high fashion.

"When we started collecting in the early 1980s, Scottish jewellery was very undervalued. It was the sort of thing your Aunt Bessie might wear on a tweed jacket."

"But these Victorian brooches and bracelets were beautifully made; the colours and textures were fabulous and I thought they would look great in a modern context."

Butler & Wilson photographed these forgotten 19th century pieces on a young model wearing a white Ralph Lauren dinner jacket and beautiful cashmere sweaters.

"Suddenly they looked fashionable again and everybody wanted them."

In the 1980s, Butler & Wilson revived Scottish jewellery for women. Today, they have created a new collection of male accessories- silver buckled belts; huge sword shaped brooches, heavy bracelets - partly inspired by these Highland ornaments.

"What I love is finding a great image from the past and adapting it for the present. I look at these pieces and I think of ancient Scottish warriors and I see my father in his Black Watch uniform."

"Celtic boys have always loved dressing up and now I'm making jewellery so that today's men can look amazing".

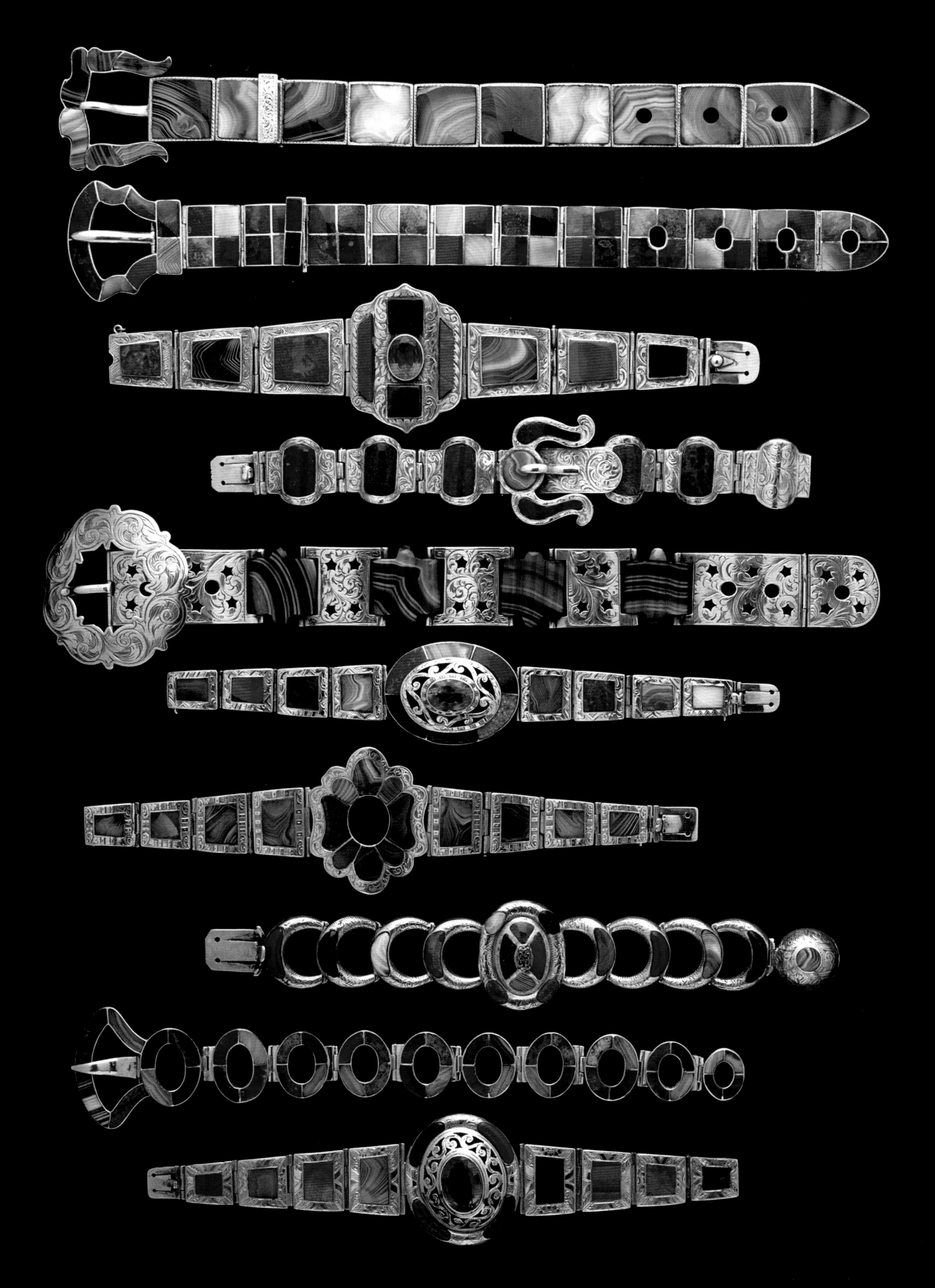

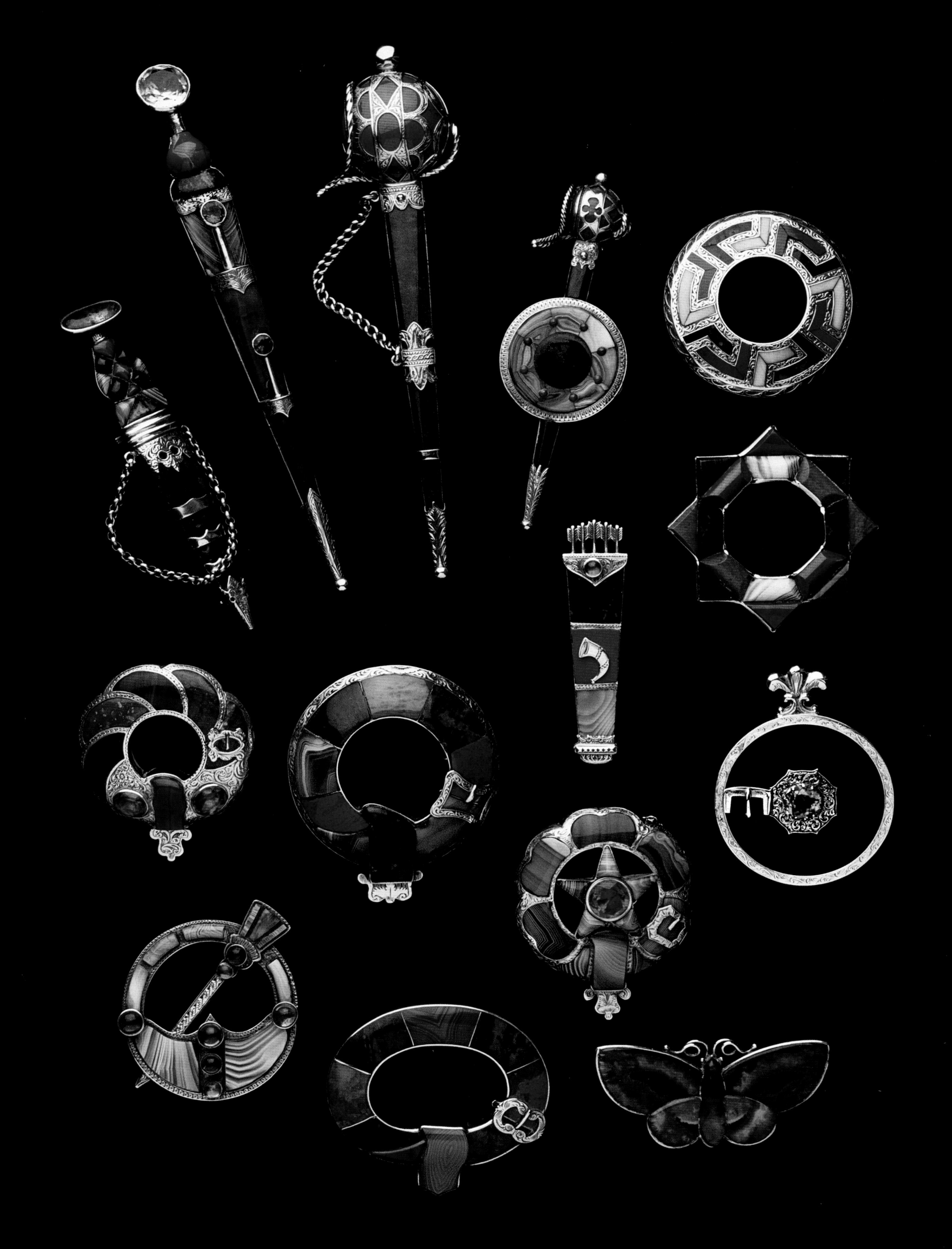

FUN AND FANTASY

"I've always loved jewellery that makes you smile. Jewellery doesn't have to be serious and you don't have to wear a big diamond to express your individuality."

Before they created their own modern designs, the first pieces of jewellery that Butler & Wilson ever manufactured were revivals of classic art deco motifs, silver and enamel brooches in the form of jazz bands, charlestoning dancers and matelots, and a series of hand-etched bakelite jewellery inspired by Pierrot.

The French version of Arlecchino, the Harlequin figure from Italian Commedia dell' Arte, Pierrot (little Peter) and his girlfriend Pierrette, were stock pantomime characters and became a favourite image in the roaring twenties.

They appeared in every medium from jewellery to ceramics to dolls and the black and white Pierrot costume was a popular fancy dress outfit, with partying bright young things.

"The Pierrot look came back in the early eighties with the New Romantics, and I've always been inspired by 1920s design."

"What I love about Art Deco is that it's timeless."

"Those clean, geometric lines look modern today, and these classic figures still conjure up a sense of fun and glamour."

"Look at the Pierrots or the diamante waiter and bellboy from our Grand Hotel series, they are stylish but they're also very charming."

Butler & Wilson's fun and fantasy designs are created in much the same spirit.

"It's about capturing feeling. Cute is a horrible word, but we've all got a sense of it."

"When you see a kitten you go "Aaah!" You can't help it!"

"What I want to do is translate that aaah factor into a piece of beautifully made jewellery."

The teddy bear is a Butler & Wilson favourite and the most popular toy of the 20th century.

The German company Steiff produced the first soft plush bears in the early 1900s, but it was the Americans who gave the bear its familiar name.

In 1902, Theodore "Teddy" Roosevelt, 26th president of the United States, was invited on a bear hunt in Mississippi.

When wild bears inconveniently neglected to appear, the embarrassed organisers tethered a baby cub to a tree and invited the president to shoot it. He famously refused this unsporting suggestion.

The incident was recorded in a newspaper cartoon, which in turn inspired a series of children's stories featuring Teddy's bears.

Toy companies leapt on the bandwagon and the teddy bear became the ultimate childhood companion.

America also pioneered children's entertainment in the 20th century.

"Thanks to film and TV we've all experienced an American childhood."

"Like most of us, I remember queuing up at the cinema when I was a kid to see the latest Disney."

Walt Disney created Mickey Mouse in 1928; and released Snow White and the Seven Dwarves 10 years later as the first US full length animated feature.

By the forties Disney charms were being produced by the leading jewellers of the world, including Cartier, and Butler & Wilson have continued this tradition with their crystal encrusted Disney brooches.

It's not just cartoon creatures that Butler & Wilson have turned into jewellery but a whole menagerie of beasts.

"Cats and dogs have always been best sellers, but over the years we have produced countless different animals."

"There is a collector for everything from owls to frogs."

"Yes, these pieces are 'cute' and funny, but we're very serious about design and quality. It's just as difficult to make a small novelty brooch as a big statement piece of jewellery, sometimes more so."

"It's very hard to capture the expression on an animal's face, or to create an articulated design that suddenly brings a figure to life. It's a long process and the detail is tremendous."

Fun and fantasy designs require both technical skill and creative imagination. "Sometimes it's about taking a traditional image and using it in a new way."

One of Butler & Wilson's first international successes was jewellery inspired by crowns and medals.

They took images of royal regalia and military decorations - abstracted these designs from their historical context - and made them into high fashion.

Giorgio Armani, king of the eighties business suit, commissioned a series of sparkling medals for his collections.

Butler & Wilson decorations were sported by celebrities from Little Richard to Tina Turner.

Ironically, these right royal fakes were so successful that when Buckingham Palace first opened its doors to the general public in 1993, Butler & Wilson were appointed to create jewellery for the Queen's gift shop.

They also supplied designs to the Tower of London, taking their crown jewels back to their original home.

"I love transforming something ordinary into something special."

"Take my rubber duck designs. I wanted to recreate that feeling you had as a kid when you played with rubber ducks in the bath, and seeing that transformed into a beautifully crafted crystal necklace – it just takes you back!"

Butler & Wilson's jewellery certainly does make you smile.

Partly it's the subjects: the kittens, the shoes, the Christmas trees, the fluffy chicks.

Partly it's the surprise of seeing these familiar images and childhood favourites turned into amazing adult jewels.

"It's got to be fun but you also have to make it beautiful."

"The whole point of jewellery like this is creating a sense of pleasure."

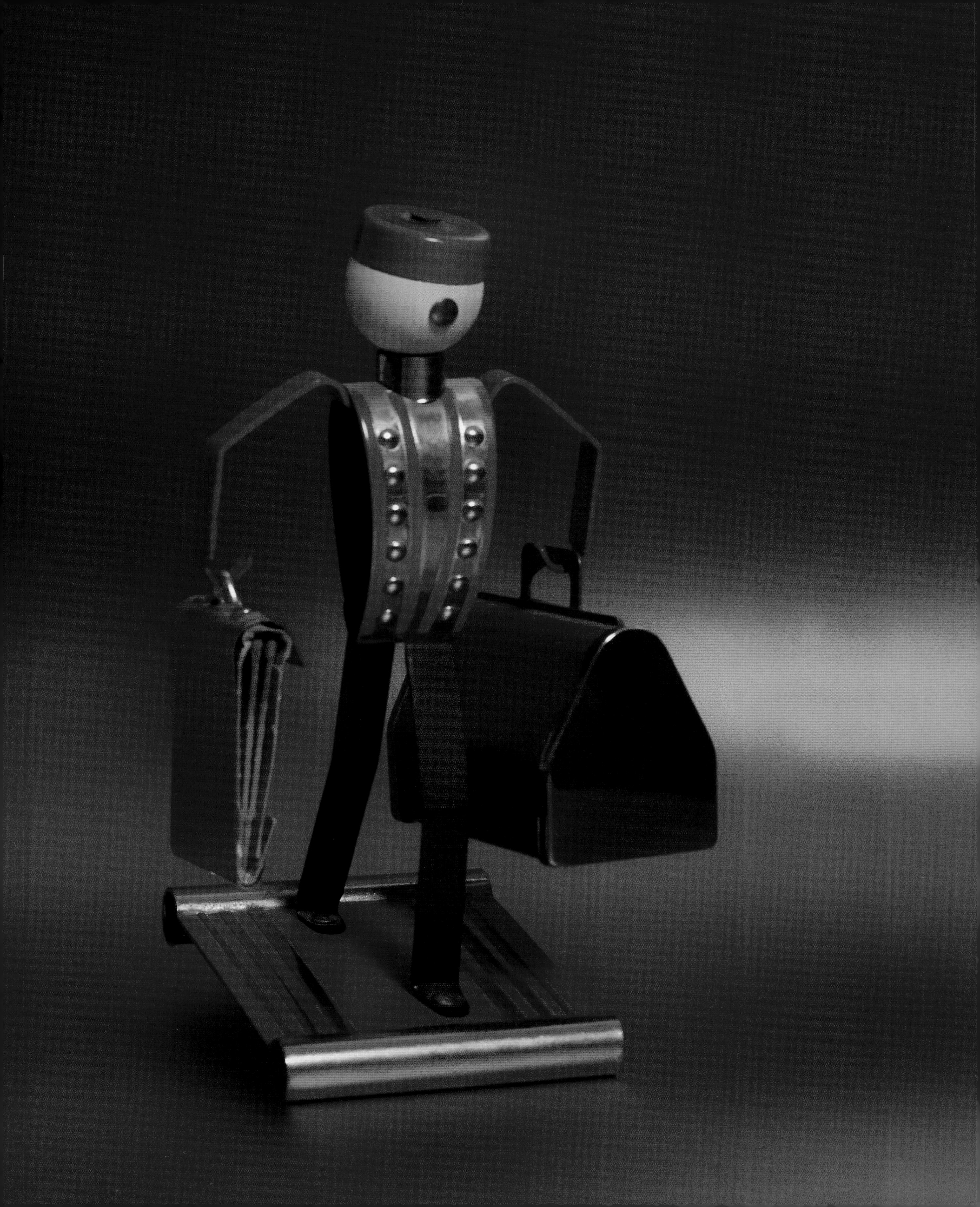

BW
BW

BUTLER & WILSON
B&W

PARIS
LA
LONDON
ROMA
NEW
RK

Carnegie
INC.

TIMMY

TRIBAL GLAMOUR

"Fashion is all about timing! It's today's young guys that inspired us to do our first collection of jewellery for Men. We noticed that they were more body conscious, obviously spending hours at the gym, skin and hair care are part of their daily routine, and adding strong masculine jewels was the finishing touch. Guys used to be dragged into our shops to choose presents for their girlfriends, now they come in to buy jewellery for themselves."

Modern men are not afraid of decorating themselves; a perfect example of this is the rise of tattooing.

The word tattoo comes from the Tahitian tatau, meaning to mark.

It first appeared in the English language in 1769, when Captain Cook discovered Tahiti and observed the islanders decorating their bodies with pierced designs.

"Everybody gets tattooed now from footballers, rock stars, and celebrities. For guys it's become a way of showing off their decorative taste and their bodies."

"Male jewellery does exactly the same thing, and today, it's an important part of our work."

Butler & Wilson's designs draw on traditional archetypes and heroic imagery.

"When I was a kid we all grew up watching westerns."

"We played cowboys and Indians and everybody wanted to be an Indian because they were the most exciting characters; they had the war paint, the feather headdresses and the best horses."

Butler & Wilson's men's jewellery brings together different influences from Navajo turquoise and silver, Asian metalwork and traditional Scottish jewellery.

Turquoise, fire opals, onyx and agates are set in heavy silver to create jewellery that is both beautiful and masculine.

"One of my favourite symbols for jewellery is the skull."

"You see it in Aztec artifacts and Mexican day of the dead pieces."

"The skull is a pure and very potent image."

"It does represent man at his most naked, but when you make it in silver, inlay it with Turquoise and Opals, you are giving it a new life and energy."

Butler & Wilson have also created jewellery for men in diamante, with designs ranging from bats to skulls to crosses, which look equally great on anything from denim to dinner jackets.

"We've come a long way from the days when the only decorations a guy could get away with were a pair of cufflinks and a tie pin."

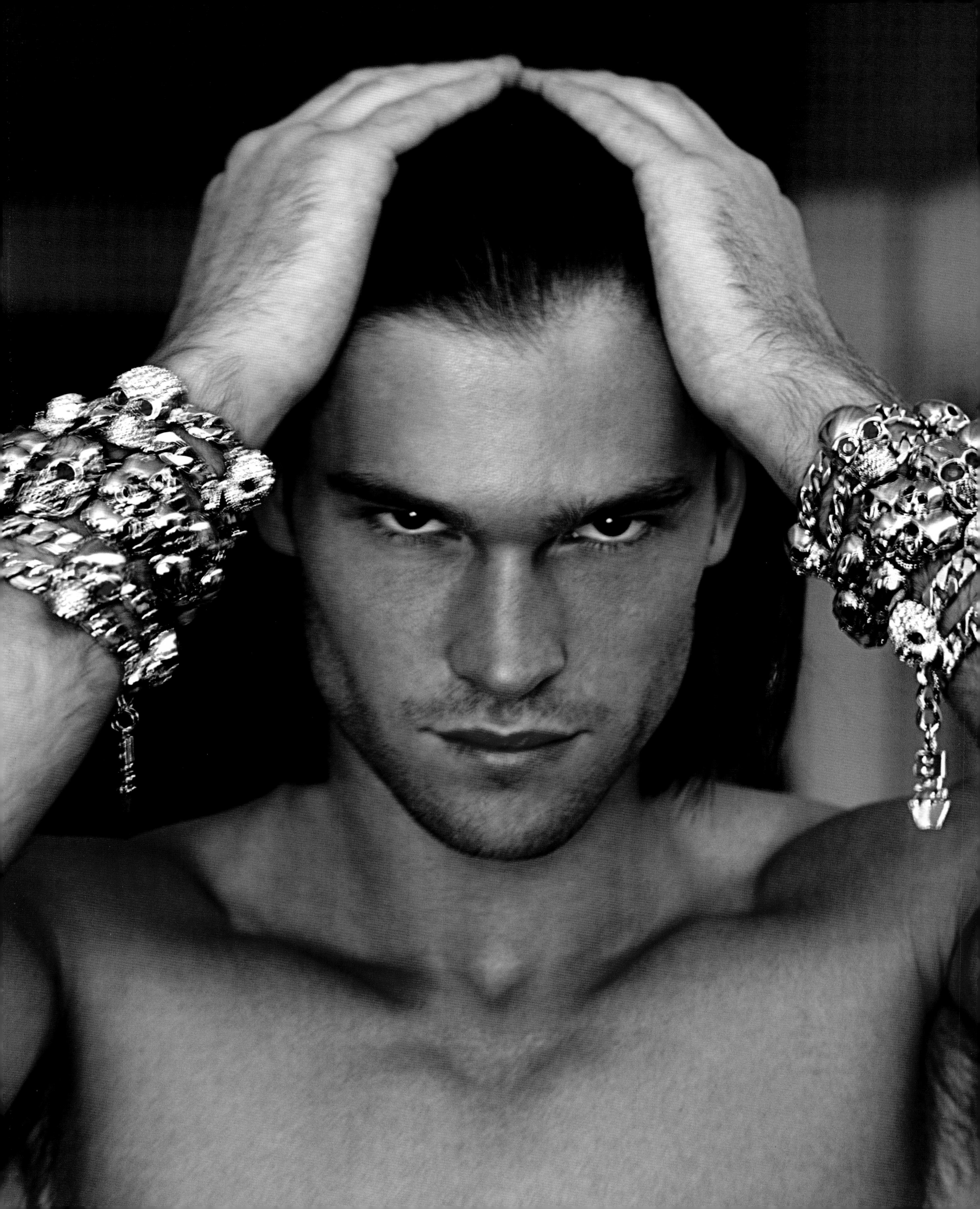

Momma

CROWN JEWELS

"Some of the most exciting jewels are those you wear on your head and the ultimate fashion statement has got to be the tiara." Decorated with diamante flowers and brilliant gemstones, Butler & Wilson's spectacular headpieces are part of a long tradition of jewellery designed to get you noticed. The tiara derives from the wreaths of real flowers and leaves that were used to celebrate power and victory in the Ancient World. The highest prize at the Olympic Games was an Olive crown; Roman emperors wore a laurel wreath to symbolize their supremacy and circlets of plants were reproduced in gold and set with precious stones to form regal diadems and tiaras.

With the collapse of Rome, the tiara fell from popularity, but it returned in the 1800s. Imitating the glories of Imperial Rome, the self-made emperor Napoleon crowned himself with a wreath of golden laurel. At their coronation, Empress Josephine wore a magnificent diamond tiara set low on her head, so that her crown could sit above it, and tiaras became the height of sparkling fashion for society ladies across Europe.

In 19th century Paris, receptions at the Russian Embassy were described as a "surging sea of tiaras". Monday and Friday at the Paris opera were declared "Soirees de diademes" – tiara nights - and even when the lights were down, the audience was illuminated with a thousand diamonds.

Showpiece jewels, tiaras typically contained the most precious family gems, often set "en tremblant" so that as a lady moved the stones shimmered and vibrated, catching the candlelight and creating a blaze of reflections round her head.

To make these expensive creations more cost effective, some were designed to be dismantled into necklaces and brooches but they had to be put back together again for formal occasions, or you could risk royal displeasure.

The Edwardian period was the golden age of tiaras which were de rigueur for royal events. At the coronation of Edward VII in 1902, the peeresses glittered with tiaras, "It seemed as if all the diamonds, sapphires, emeralds and rubies in the empire were on exhibition," reported the New York Times.

Edward made it mandatory that when debutantes were presented at court, young girls should wear three Prince of Wales white feathers in their hair, whilst their mothers and married women should sport a tiara.

His daughter in law Queen Mary was another stickler for formal jewellery and even when dining alone with George V or her children, would always put on one of her many tiaras.

Tiaras were still being worn by the British Aristocracy in the 1920s and 30s, but times and tastes were changing. With growing informality after WWII (Queen Elizabeth abolished court presentation of debutantes in 1958), it appeared the tiara was finished, but thanks in part to Butler & Wilson, it wasn't.

In the early 1990s, the fashion world was turned upside down by a new trend. "Grunge" was in, dressing up was out, and washing your hair was optional.

To most jewellers, this spelled disaster. How does one glamorize dressing-down?

For Butler & Wilson, it meant an opportunity to, as always, dictate trends rather than follow them. "People get married no matter what and they always want to look fantastic on their wedding day. So we decided to bring back the tiara."

Sparkling defiantly in the face of hard times, Butler & Wilson's crystal tiaras were an instant success and yet again the company had pioneered a new fashion.

Tiaras became a bridal must have and party favourite with the new popocracy of rock-stars and celebrities.

Elton John's "White Tie and Tiara" charity balls were the social events of the season and in 2002 the Victoria and Albert Museum held a famous exhibition of tiaras, in which historic headdresses belonging to empresses and queens sparkled alongside new creations by Vivienne Westwood and Butler & Wilson.

"Formal occasions might have largely disappeared but people still want to look fabulous. Girls wear these decorations for weddings, parties, clubbing and just for fun. Tiaras are the most dramatic of all jewels and the essence of dressing up."

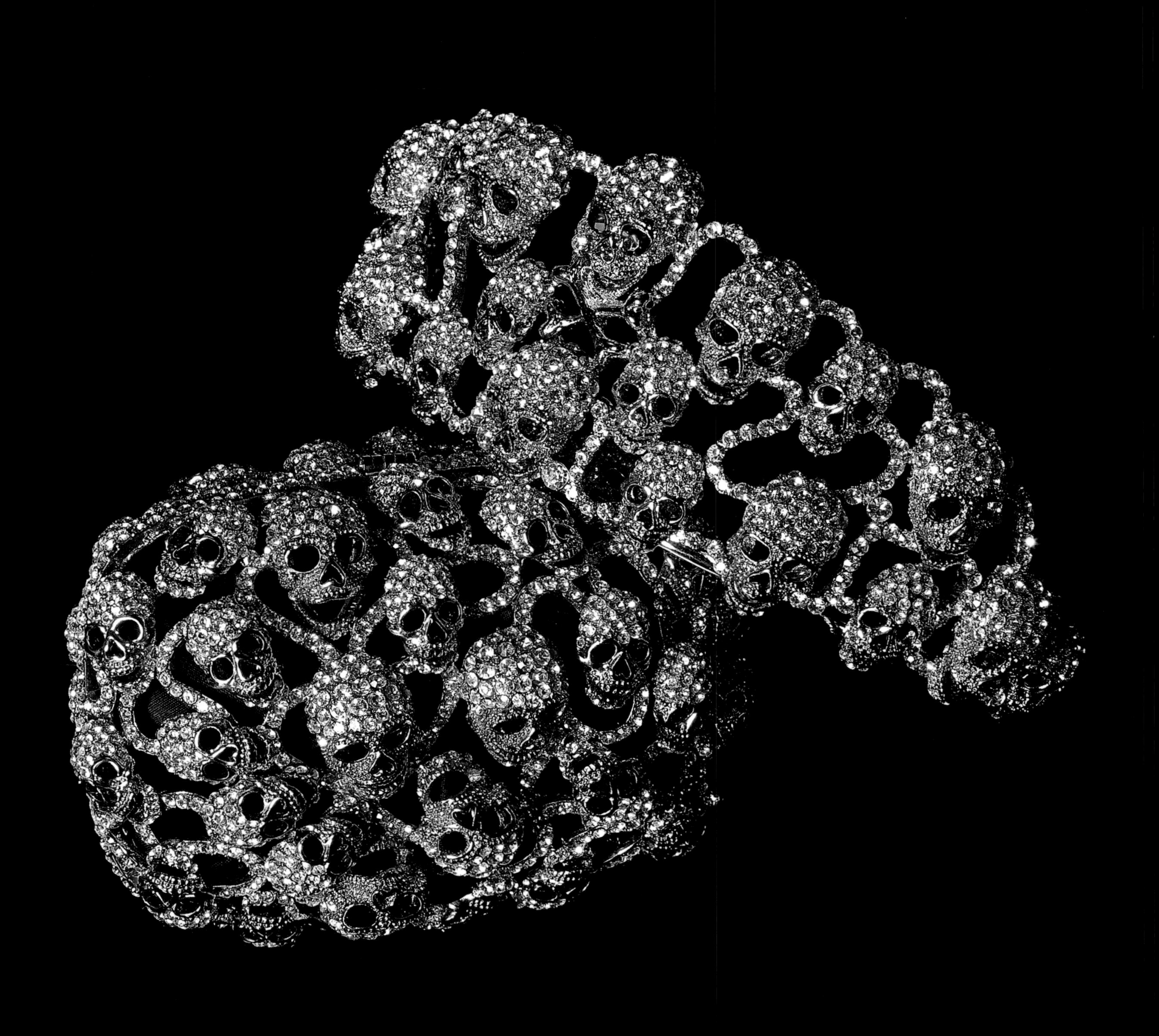

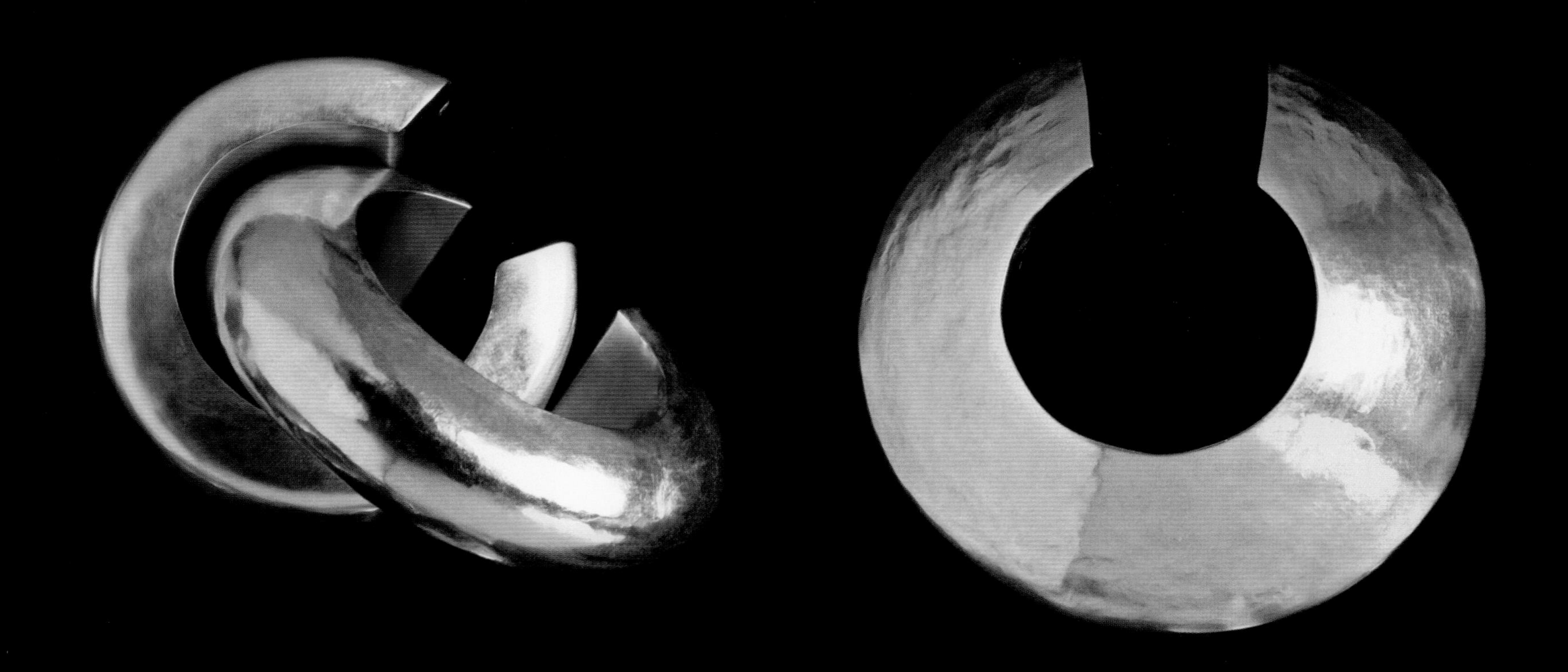

"Nikky, an exotic beauty
who has always
amazed and inspired"

HISTORY

1969 Butler & Wilson was established when Nicky Butler & Simon Wilson begin selling Antique jewellery from their stand in the Antiquarius Market in the Kings Road, Chelsea.

1972 First shop opened on the Fulham Road.

1975 First original designs added to Art Deco Collection.

1979 Simon is commissioned to design The Regent Street Christmas Lights, which prove so successful that they are used again in 1980.

1982 Fulham Road Shop is expanded including the launch of the famous billboards featuring many of the world's most beautiful women, including Catherine Deneuve, Faye Dunaway, Charlotte Rampling, and Jerry Hall.

1984 Commissioned by The Pirelli Company to create a unique and glamorous collection for its famous calendar.

Commission to design an exclusive range of jewellery for the Giorgio Armani Collection.

1985 Second shop is opened in the fashionable South Molton Street, in the heart of London's West End.

1986 First outlet, a concession in Harrods, Knightsbridge, opens.

1988 Nicky Butler moves to Los Angeles to launch the first international shop on Sunset Boulevard, Hollywood.

Margaret Wilson opens store in Prince's Square Glasgow.

1989 21st anniversary celebrations with a major retrospective exhibition in Harrods Department store.

1990 The launch of the 'Rough Diamonds' book documenting the company's history, highlighting the dramatic changes in jewellery fashions.

1994 Joins QVC, the shopping channel, which starts a hugely successful partnership.

Designed an Imperial Jewellery Collection, for The Tower of London's Jewel House shop.

Buckingham Palace opens to the public for the first time. Appointed to design a range of jewellery inspired by the details of the interior of the Palace.

1997 Renovation of the Fulham Road shop to extend the collections to include Vintage Clothes & Handbags, and the Butler & Wilson Bridal Jewellery Collection.

1998 Simon joins Swarovski to give a lecture tour of Bangkok, Hong Kong, Tokyo, and Seoul.

1999 30th Anniversary Celebrations, with a charity Gala Dinner and fashion show at the Natural History Museum, South Kensington, in aid of the Royal Marsden Hospital.

2000 B&W World launched, introducing a range of handbags and clothing to add to the existing jewellery collection.

2002 Semi Precious range introduced, including opal, turquoise, onyx. It's big, bold, and beautiful.

2004 First collaboration with the famous US lingerie label Victoria's Secret for their fashion shows.

2005 Men's Jewellery Collection launched, blending silver with semi precious stones, becoming an instant success.

2006 Creation of jewel encrusted exclusive Couture Bags, Pure Luxury.

2007 Beautiful Beaded Wedding Dresses added to Bridal Collection in Fulham Road store.

2009 Refurbishment of South Molton Street Store, and introduction of 70s and 80s vintage clothing.

Butler & Wilson's 40 book published.

40th Anniversary party and fashion show at KOKO's in aid of Breast Cancer Care.

THANK YOU

To my sister Margaret, who has organised my mad life and has always been there for me. I love you.

To Noi, whose love and friendship has provided a home away from home.

To Wei Hou Chen and Li Jun Xie, for helping me create beautiful jewellery and always looking after me.

To Boy and Pu, for not only producing gorgeous jewellery, but also bringing little August into our family.

To James, for your tenacity, creativity, and hard work.

To everyone at Volume magazine, especially Looknam, one of the most creative make up artists I have ever worked with, Tu for his friendship and all the latest gossip, and Anon for his inspiration.

To Colin for his insight, terrific photos, and for taking the time.

To Madeleine for putting my thoughts into words.

To Tik and Ning for their genius.

To Miss Mei Yu Lin for her fabulous jewels, and the great tea.

To Ray for his friendship and great parties.

To Isr for his wonderful styling and creative vision.

To Chicken for all the great ideas.

To Elaine Bosson, we did some great things together.

To Paola and Jacques, for over 30 years of friendship.

To all the fashion editors and magazines who have supported us from the very beginning.

To all the amazing photographers and models we've worked with over the years.

To QVC and Breast Cancer Care for their support.

To Ana Paula Junqueira, Andrea Dellal, and Monica Cordosa for all their help with our fundraising.

To our amazing customers for enjoying our designs and having fun.

And finally, to all the girls and staff at Butler & Wilson, past and present, who help to make our stores the best in London.

Your love and support has helped me through the good times and the bad.

I couldn't have done it without you.

Bettine
Photo by Barry Lategan
Make Up by Arianne Poole

Photo © Colin Roy

Shoes by Butler & Wilson
Jan
Photo by Dear

Shoes by Butler & Wilson
Jan
Photo by Dear

Jet Girls

Victorian Lady
Wearing Jet Jewellery

Photo by Uli Weber

Antique Jet Jewellery
Photo by Tom Dawes &
Prudence Cummings Associates

Toko
Photo by John Swannell

Antique Jet Jewellery
Photo © Colin Roy

Antique French Glass Jewellery
Leon
Photo © Colin Roy

Photo by Uli Weber

Celtic Boys

Hector Wilson
Simon's Dad

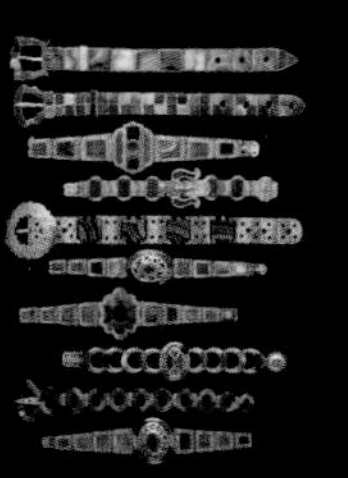

Morgan
Photo © Colin Roy
Styling by Isr Upa-In

Victorian Scottish Bracelets
Photo by Tom Dawes &
Prudence Cummings Associates

Morgan
Photo © Colin Roy
Styling by Isr Upa-In

Butler & Wilson Fire Opal & Onyx
Photo © Colin Roy

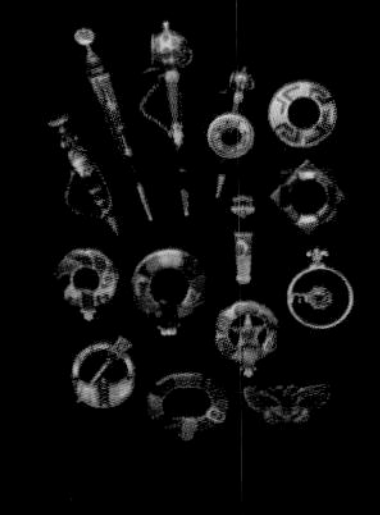

Victorian Scottish Pins
Photo by Tom Dawes &
Prudence Cummings Ass

Morgan
Photo © Colin Roy
Styling by Isr Upa-In

Fun & Fantasy
Vintage Butler & Wilson
Frog Brooch

Vintage Butler & Wilson
Galalite Pierrots

Fun & Fantasy
Vintage Butler & Wilson
Monkey Brooch

Butler & Wilson Brooches
Photo © Colin Roy

Vintage Butler & Wilson
Bellboy Brooches
Photo © Colin Roy

South Molton Street
Photo © Colin Roy

Photos © Colin Roy

Photos © Colin Roy

Flower Painting by Chris J

Photos © Colin Roy

Antique Prince Matchab
Perfume Bottle
Vintage Trifari Crown Pin
Photo © Colin Roy

Butler & Wilson Brooches
Photo © Colin Roy

Dress & Shoes Butler & Wilson
Anstasia
Photo by Dear

Ksusha
Photo by Dear

Images Courtesy
Vogue Hommes Japan
Photos by Sølve Sundsbø
Styling by Nicola Formichetti

Dress by Butler & Wilson
Photo by Dear
Hair by Liliane Sri-Eard (Lili)

Photo by Dear
Hair by Lili

Alian
Photo © Colin Roy

Alian
Photo © Colin Roy

Vintage YSL Dress
Photo by Dear

The Miracle of Flowers

Bettine
Photo by Barry Lategan
Make Up by Arianne Poole

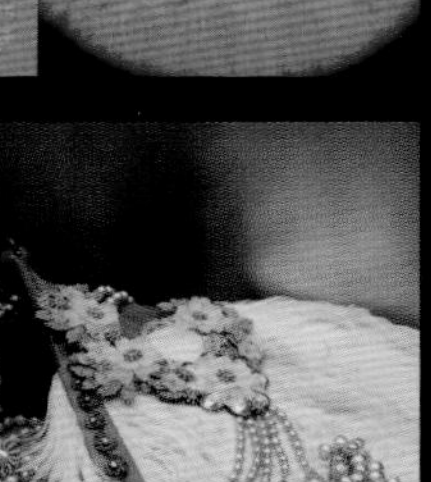

1950s Lucite Bag
Vintage Stanley Hagler Jewellery
Photo © Colin Roy

Photo © Colin Roy

Nikky Akhtar & Rahini
Photo by Angus Ross

Patricia Having Simon for Dinner
Photo by Termsit

Flower Painting by Chris James
Photo © Colin Roy

Bibi
Photo by Termsit

Photo © Colin Roy

Vintage Stanley Hagler Jewellery
Photo © Colin Roy

Vinny
Photo by Termsit

Antique Liberty Dressing Gown
Photo © Colin Roy

Photo © Colin Roy

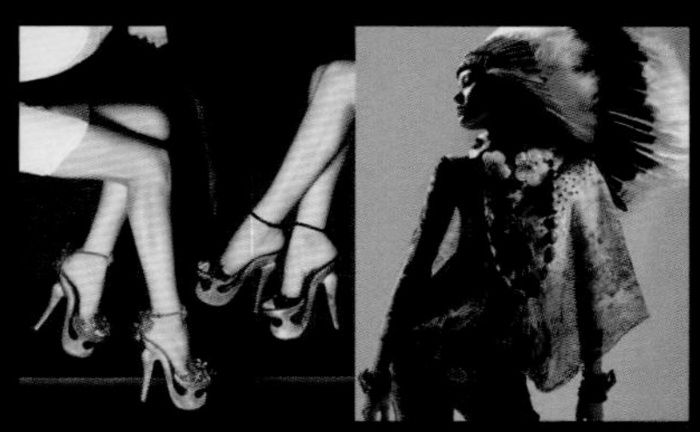

Butler & Wilson Shoes
Photo by Dear
Hair by Lili

Photo by Tada Varich

Vintage Waldy Bags
Photo © Colin Roy

Photo © Colin Roy

Photo © Colin Roy

Ali Rhodes
Photo © Colin Roy

Butler & Wilson Couture Bag
Photo by Dear

Bibi
Photo by Termsit

Butler & Wilson Couture Bag
Photo © Colin Roy

Opal Jewels
Photo © Colin Roy

Kanyanut Bamrungpong (Alian)
by Thananon Thanakornkarn (Dear)
Make Up by Sukhon Srimarattanakul (Looknam)

Photo by Dear

Dedication to Christina Wilson
Simon's Mum

Alian
by Dear
Make Up by Looknam

Jewelled Box
Photos © Colin Roy

Photo by John Swannell

Dazzling Diamante
All Text by Madeleine Marsh

Toko
Photo by John Swannell

Dazzling Diamante

Rahini
Photo by Angus Ross

Patricia
Photo by Termsit Siriphanich

1950s Lucite Bag
Photo © Colin Roy

Maria Luisa
by John Swannell

Dancing Couple Brooch
Photo by Dear

Diamante Lizard Brooches
Photo by Tom Dawes &
Prudence Cummings Associates

Alian
Photo by Dear
Styling by Isr Upa-In

Bibi
Photo by Termsit

Vinny
Photo by Termsit

Alian
Photo by Dear

Photo by Tom Dawes &
Prudence Cummings Associate

Ksusha
Photo by Dear

Alian
Photo by Termsit

Nikica
Photo by Termsit

Elena
Photo by Dear

Photo © Colin Roy

Vintage Butler & Wilson Dress
Alian
Photo © Colin Roy

Vintage Butler & Wilson Dress
Alian
Photo © Colin Roy

Couture Bag Butler & Wilson
Photo by Dear

Photo by Tom Dawes &
Prudence Cummings Associate

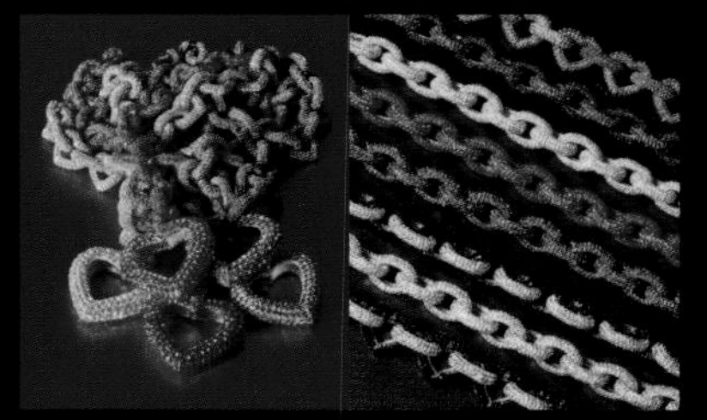

Diamante Heart Necklaces
Photo © Colin Roy

Diamante Necklaces
Photo © Colin Roy

Vintage Moschino Suit
Anstasia & Jan
Photo by Dear

Skull Box & Tiara
Photo © Colin Roy

Morgan
Photo © Colin Roy

Jan
Photo by Dear

Isabella
Photo by Dear

Rahini
Photo by Angus Ross

Paola & Jacques for Butler & Wilson
Rahini
Photo By Angus Ross

Tiaras
Photo © Colin Roy

Photo by Dear

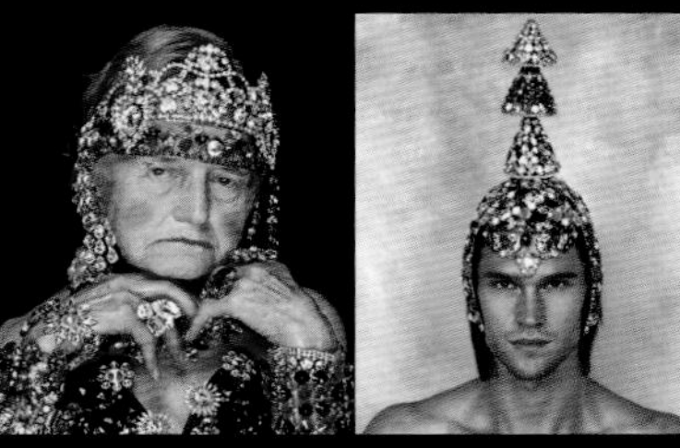

Emily Perry
Dame Edna's Maid Madge Allsop
28 June 1907 – 19 February 2008
Photo by Trevor Leighton

Leon
Photo © Colin Roy

Nikky Akhtar
Simon's P.A.
Photo by Green & Russell

E-Kollection for Butler & Wilson

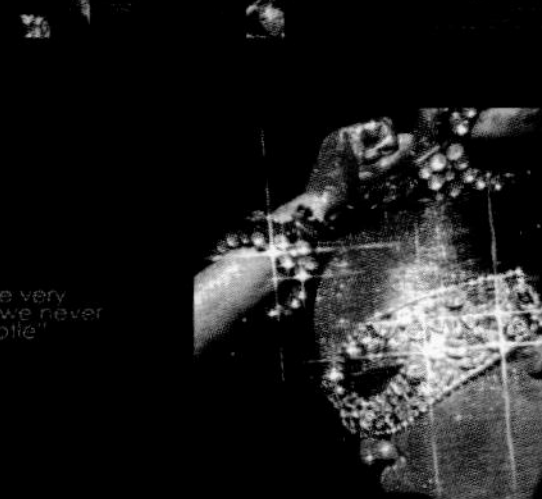

Alian
Photo by Dear

Butler & Wilson Stores

20 South Molton Street
LONDON W1K 5QY
TEL: 020 7409 2955

189 Fulham Road
LONDON SW3 6JN
TEL: 020 7352 3045

www.butlerandwilson.co.uk
enquiries@butlerandwilson.co.uk

Madeleine Marsh is a writer and broadcaster specialising in antiques and social history. For many years she was the editor of Miller's Collectables Price Guide and she has written a number of books including Collecting the 1950s and Collecting the 1960s. Madeleine is an expert on the BBC Antiques Roadshow and has appeared on many television programmes. She has lectured across the world on vintage fashion and accessories.

First Published in Great Britain in 2009 by
Butler & Wilson Ltd
189 Fulham Road
LONDON SW3 6JN

ISBN 978-0-9561483-0-8

Colour Separation Soontornfilm Co Limited Bangkok
Printed by Sirivatana Interprint Public Co Ltd Bangkok

Photo by Tada

Silver Turquoise Opals
Photo © Colin Roy

Vinny
Photo by Termsit

Belt Buckles
Photo by Dear

Photos by Tada

Silver & Turquoise
Photo © Colin Roy

Mateus
Photo by Termsit
Tattoos by Arkom Sombuttham

Mateus
Photos by Termsit
Tattoos by Arkom Sombuttham

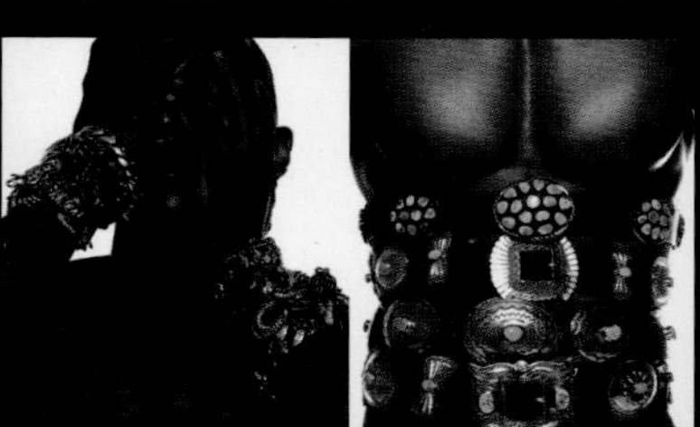

Collins
Photo by Dear

Collins
Photo by Dear

Dejvis
Photo by Dear

Hugo
Photo by Termsit

Andy
Photo © Colin Roy

Turquoise
Photo © Colin Roy

Dejvis
Photo by Dear

Jan
Photo by Dear
Make Up by Looknam

Jan
Photo by Dear
Make Up by Looknam

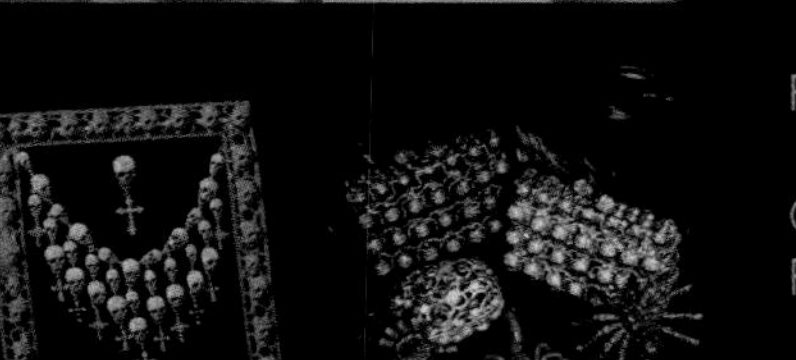

Photo © Colin Roy

Couture Bag, Brooches, & Box
Photo © Colin Roy

Nikica
Photo by Termsit

Wally
First Male Billboard
Photo by Rod Nissen-Petzer

Jan
Photo by Dear

Jan
Photo by Dear

Jan
Photo by Dear

Jan
Photo by Dear

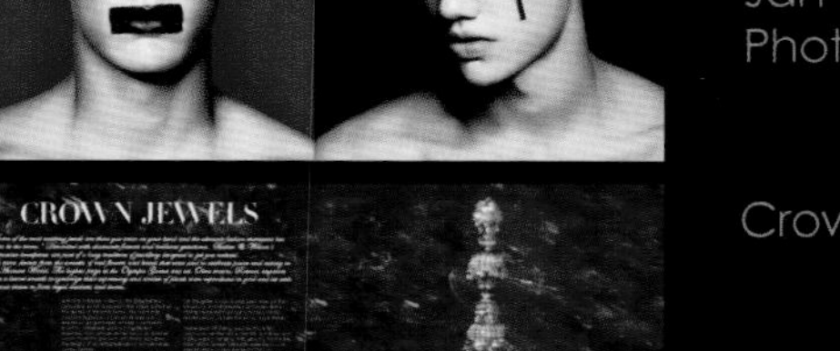

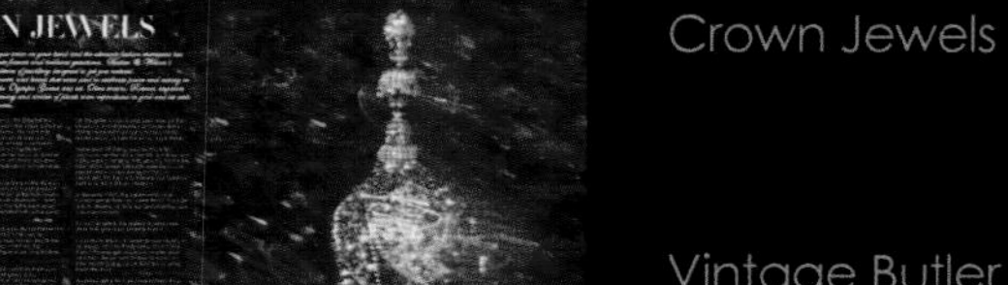

Crown Jewels

Vintage Butler & Wilson Headdress
Photo © Colin Roy

Antique Lace
Elena
Photo by Dear

Ali Rhodes
Photo © Colin Roy

Antique Lace
Elena
Photo by Dear

Antique Lace
Elena
Photo by Dear

Ksusha
Photo by Dear

Anstasia
Photo by Dear
Make Up by Looknam

Anstasia
Photo by Dear
Make Up by Looknam

Photos © Colin Roy

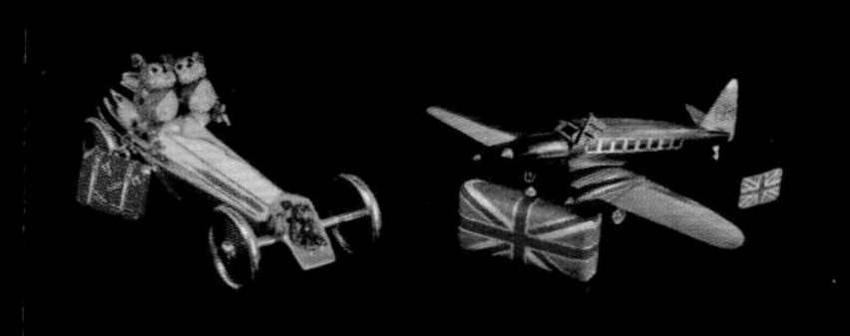

Photos © Colin Roy

Picture Frames
Photos © Colin Roy

Photo © Colin Roy

Disney Brooches by
Butler & Wilson
Page Design James Felton

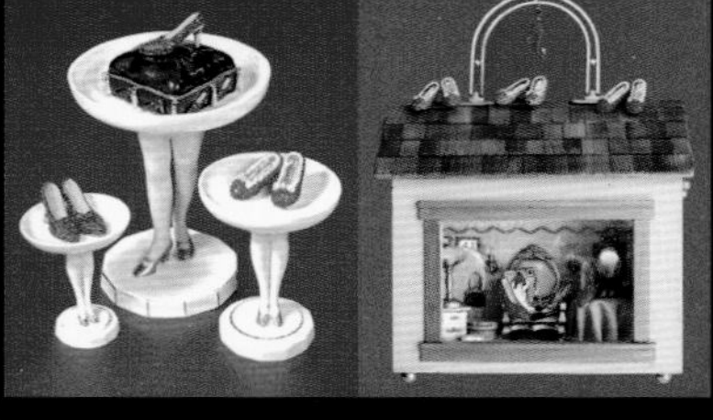

Photo © Colin Roy

Vintage Doll's House Handbag
Photo © Colin Roy

Dejvis
Photo by Dear

Abiste Crystal Duck Bag for
Butler & Wilson
Photo © Colin Roy

Photo by Dear

Photo by Dear
Hair by Lili

Antique Cappo Di Monte Owl
Photo © Colin Roy

Photo © Colin Roy

Photos © Colin Roy

Timmy

Crab Trinket Box
Photo © Colin Roy

Catharine
Photo by Dear

Photos © Colin Roy

Tribal Glamour

Tibetan Skull
Photo © Colin Roy

Leon
Photo © Colin Roy

Morgan
Photo by Dear

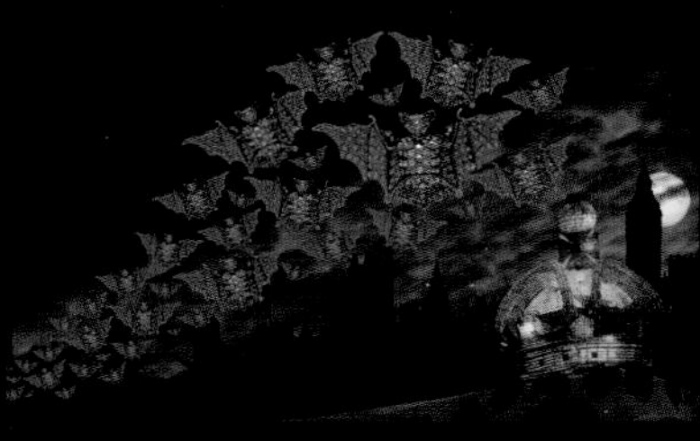

Crown on
Fulham Road Shop
Crown Photo © Colin Roy
Page Design James Felton

Leon
The Face of Butler & Wilson
Men's Collection
Photos © Colin Roy

Antique Tibetan Artefacts
Photo © Colin Roy

Leon
Photo © Colin Roy

Photo © Colin Roy

Mateus
Photo by Termsit

"From the very beginning, we never did subtle"